SELF-LOVE WORKBOOK FOR WOMEN

Overcome Low Self Esteem & Supercharge Your
Self-Love With Daily Habits, Affirmations,
Self Discovery Practices & Much More

Relove Psychology

FREE GIFT

Greetings!

First of all, we want to thank you for reading our books. We aim to create the very best books for our readers.

Now we invite you to join our exclusive list. As a subscriber, you will receive a free gift, weekly tips, free giveaways, discounts and so much more.

All of this is 100% free with no strings attached!

To claim your bonus simply head to the link below or scan the QR code below.

RELOVEPSYCHOLOGY

https://www.subscribepage.com/relovepsychology

Table of Contents

Introduction

On March 8, 2021, The Body Shop launched a global report that revealed a dilemma haunting women all over the world: There is a self-love crisis that needs to be addressed urgently. The report, which ran for two months and surveyed over 22,000 people from 21 different countries revealed, that one in two women feel more self-doubt than self-love, and 60% of them wish they had more respect for themselves. (Mustafa, 2021).

Of course, we all go through days where we just feel numb. Our self-confidence hits a dip, we worry about the future, and also struggle to forgive ourselves for our past mistakes. However, these feelings of inadequacy should not linger long enough to affect our overall well-being and daily functionalities.

As a woman, when you're going through a crisis like this, you feel pleasure in neglecting yourself. You wake up every day thinking about ways you can avoid people. What's the point of being social if you're going to be awkward, anyway? Furthermore, you're having financial pressures from all angles of your life, so you have plenty of things to stress about. Then, there's the excruciating pain of having to quickly glance past the mirror every time you come across it because you don't feel too beautiful, and you cannot stand the shape of your body.

No matter how many times you try, things never seem to go your way. You feel stuck, always feeling like you need to work twice as hard to achieve even the simplest things. You are a failure who constantly thinks about the mistakes they've made in their past and how you're going to repeat them, anyway. To be honest, you feel a bit too ashamed for being such a disappointment. If there is anything you're certain about right now, it's that you do not deserve anything that might dare present itself to you.

The funny thing about self-perception is that it does not allow you to broaden your knowledge. Once you take something as a fact, it becomes your gospel truth. What is even more intriguing about this is that although you have adopted these negative concepts about yourself to be nothing but the truth, you still yearn for something different.

So, you know you're neglecting yourself, yet you keep on denying yourself the opportunity to just be good to yourself! You get so many compliments throughout the day, but you just feel guilty for accepting statements that feel like a joke.

You want to be like other women and have the ability to look in the mirror and embrace most, if not every, part of yourself. Remember, there was a time when you could do that, so what's stopping you now? You miss the bolder, and more courageous version of you that used to believe that she could make her dreams come true. You had a more positive outlook on life, and you'd constantly look into the future with confidence. You spend every day of your life wondering if it's possible to turn your life around and embrace a more fulfilling life. The answer is yes, it's true, and this book is going to show you how.

It all starts with self-love. That is, a state of appreciation and regard for one's own happiness and capabilities. Without it, you only go through life as if you're just here to be an extra on a high-end classic movie. Everyone else is claiming their story, but you're just standing there in the background and observing. Firstly, this book is going to teach you how to understand this powerful concept by building your self-esteem. You are going to face the uncomfortable truths that you've been avoiding for so long, so that you may embark on a journey of building a different, truthful, and pleasant opinion of yourself.

Then, through compelling, practical, and enjoyable exercises, you're going to learn how to put yourself first! This means learning to define what it is that you really want and then going out there to communicate it most effectively. There will be no more feeling guilty about it, no more saying yes when you want to say no, and definitely no more neglecting your needs for the sake of others.

While it might sound like a foreign concept, I'm going to teach you how to be gentle with yourself. You will no longer use harsh words, punishments, and unforgiveness to torture your precious soul. The love you give so freely to your loved ones is something you are going to do for yourself. Sounds scary? Well, it shouldn't, I believe you can do this!

Finally, through the power of your thoughts, words, and actions, I'm going to show you how powerful you are. Yes, you! The things you allow your mind to focus on slowly become a reality. Your words, coupled with these harmful thoughts, drive you to influence actions that harm you. While you might've enjoyed doing this in the past, the time has come for you to use these elements differently! Just as much as you've focused your energy in the past to create negative realities, we are now going to take a different direction and I can guarantee you, it's going to be empowering.

Your days of self-loathing are over. In every chapter, some exercises are going to move you closer to a state of mind that you deserve to experience. Embrace them, enjoy them, and allow yourself to transition into the beautiful individual you've always known you are.

This book landed in your life for a reason, so how about we get started on this exciting journey?

Are you ready to show yourself some love?

CHAPTER 1: Putting Yourself First

It's not selfish, but selfless to be first, to be as good as possible to you, to take care of you, to keep you whole and healthy, that doesn't mean that you disregard everything and everyone, but you gotta keep your cup full.

— Iyanla Vanzant

The idea of putting yourself first is scary, I get it. When you've never allowed yourself to do something as courageous as that, of course, it's going to feel like a foreign concept that should never be explored. Well, that's a completely natural belief to hold. However, it's 100% untrue and if the heading of this chapter made you feel weird, then it's a perfect sign you need to continue reading!

This chapter is all about learning to make yourself the priority for once! It's about learning to think about what you truly want, how to communicate your needs, and how you can get started on ensuring that you emphasize more importance to the things you've always been yearning for.

Putting yourself first is a strong indicator of communicating self-love to yourself. After all, there is power in the word "self!" Before we start putting you first, let's first look at why and how you got to a point where putting yourself first became a scary concept to follow.

There's no denying that women have a long generational history of having their needs silenced. Even as the years have gone by and times have changed, it still isn't easy to communicate our needs and expectations. In an intimate relationship it's called nagging, at work it's called being difficult, at school they call it being lazy, and in family settings, it's called being needy. Furthermore, there's been a damning belief that nurturing comes instinctively to women. While that is true, society has misinterpreted this fact and allowed the concept to run around the idea that women should be giving love and not necessarily receiving it. Being the gentle creatures that we are, we've allowed this idea to linger as long as it has, but we still feel the natural need to have softness and tenderness ushered to us. Now, there are three important points that we need to discuss that are preventing us from embracing the concept of prioritizing ourselves:

1. We believe it exposes us as being selfish.

To be selfish means to lack consideration for other people. However, how many times have you been blown away by the way people have no issues with putting themselves first? You're probably struggling too.

When it comes to the concept of self-love, it's the people who love you most that will encourage you to look out for yourself. They will be the first to let you know that you should take a break when they can see you're tired. They'll offer to help you out when you're overwhelmed, and they won't hesitate to put their own lives on pause just to make sure that you're okay.

2. We think it means neglecting other people.

Putting yourself first does not mean taking care of yourself and only you alone! It simply means that if you've got five things to do every day, you need to ensure that you're on top of the list or if there are six people that you need to feed, then you feed yourself first.

I know most people are scared to embark on this journey because they are concerned it will mean not showing up for other people. But this concept simply challenges you to consider whether you're giving people so much attention that you end up neglecting your own needs. Are you spending the entire day doing favors for people that by the time you get home you're frustrated and mad at yourself for not doing anything that could've benefited you? If your answer is yes, then you need to reconsider how you show up for yourself.

3. We believe we need to get it from people!

The most important point in this chapter! No matter how much people love you, they're never going to stop you from prioritizing them in your life. Yes, you expect your aunt to understand that you can't keep driving her to her doctor's appointment during your work hours, but if you always offer, she won't turn you down. Do you know that friend that always shakes your budget by always asking you for money that she never pays back? She's not going to stop asking and she won't get into the habit of paying you back either because you don't communicate that it's problematic for you.

In other words, putting yourself first is your sole responsibility. A lot of people stop trying to put themselves first because they're overwhelmed by the amount of reliance that other people have on them. While that's understandable to a certain agree, you need to start being firm about adjusting your priorities in a way that will benefit you before it benefits anyone else!

So, how are you supposed to ensure that you put yourself first by tackling the points we've just discussed? By practicing positive actions that tackle these issues objectively. If you want to deal with being considerate of others, then consider putting yourself first by establishing boundaries. If you were under the impression that you need to get permission from people to put yourself first, then you'll need to focus on practicing self-care and finally, if you're still adamant about serving others, then I'd like to introduce you to purposeful living!

Before we uncover these important points, you need to get comfortable with the practice of journaling. In this workbook, you're going to allow yourself to engage in the exercises and answer all questions asked. You might be tempted to document your progress in other ways such as recording voice notes, or videos, however, writing it down in your workbook should still be your first choice. Journaling is going to benefit your overall well-being and help you achieve any goal you set for yourself. In 2018, Cambridge University Press published a research article regarding the emotional and physical health benefits of expressive writing. The participants were asked to write about emotional, stressful, or traumatic events that they'd experienced in their lives. On three to five occasions, they were required to document their thoughts for 15-20 minutes.

Although the participants reported emotional trauma and being upset while journaling, they found the exercise valuable and meaningful. Furthermore, they reported reduced depressive symptoms, altered social behavior, and improved self-esteem. (Baikie & Wilhelm, 2005).

Throughout these chapters, you'll be required to participate in journaling as well. No matter how upsetting it might get for you on some occasions, always remember that you'll walk away with improved problem-solving skills, a greater appreciation of your reality, and a clearer mind!

It's Time to Set Boundaries

Although there are multiple aspects involved in this topic, you need to understand that there is nothing more courageous than setting boundaries. It lets the people around you know that there is a certain way that you deserve to be treated and that there will be consequences should your needs be ignored. Internally, it indicates that you know you're worth the good treatment and are more than willing to make sacrifices that will bring you peace and happiness.

Looking at your relationships at home, work, and in your social circle, boundaries are the invisible lines that will separate you from other people. This separation comes in the form of protection from harmful words, actions, and thoughts that will deny you the opportunity to love yourself.

Some women struggle with communicating their needs, others want to learn how to say no more often, and others just don't know what do to when people ignore this invisible line. The bottom line is that boundaries are an indication of love and improve your relationships in the long run. Think about this: if someone loves and respects you, they will ensure that they don't cross that line. And this applies to you. You've got to love yourself hard enough to respect your preferences and you've got to hold yourself accountable every time you allow people to ignore your boundaries. Of course, this line can change or be adjusted over time, but that should only be done willingly, by you!

When you cannot set boundaries, you become frustrated, sometimes even angry, and this can confuse the people around you because they see you offering to do things for them, but they don't understand why it makes you angry. However, the more you teach them how you want to be treated, the easier it becomes for them to cater to your needs. This kind of respect is going to ensure that you and they are always on the same page, which will be a great thing for your relationships.

Exercise 1: What Do I Want?

Now that we've established that boundaries are important even for people like us, who struggle to communicate effectively. I'd like you to guide every exercise you're going to participate in by firstly being sure of what you truly want. While it might be easier to focus on what you *don't* want, it's much more powerful to be specific about the kind of reality you want to create for yourself because it's going to propel you to take an active lead in redirecting your life and the way you feel about yourself.

Below are the top aspects of your life that are at risk of being taken advantage of. Unsurprisingly, they are linked to your fundamental rights as a human, but because you've spent such a long time downplaying your value, you did not notice that you were allowing the world to gradually take your rights away from you.

In these departments of your life, you're going to identify the key elements that will ensure that none of your boundaries is crossed and that you'll be able to clearly articulate what you want. To analyze boundaries more effectively, ask yourself, *What are my rights in this aspect of my life?* Your rights! Not what the constitution says, what your culture says, or what your parents or loved ones enforced on you. This is all about you and what feels right in your body, mind, and soul!

1. Your sexuality
2. Your possessions and physical space (i.e., your house, room, or office space)
3. Your body
4. Your time
5. Your energy and emotions
6. Beliefs, attitudes, and opinions
7. Values and moral compass

Once you've written them down, I'd like you to reflect on how this exercise made you feel by writing a journal entry below. Identify your emotions and investigate why you felt that way. Did you feel shameful for saying you have the right to choose who you want to be with? Is it because homosexuality is still a foreign concept in your family? Did talking about how you want to spend your time make you feel angry because you currently feel bullied in your life? The ability to embrace these emotions and how they affect you regularly is what is going to empower you to complete the second exercise below.

_____

_____

_____

_____

_____

_____

_____

_____

_____

Exercise 2: The Month of No!

For the next month, you're going to address the biggest issue that comes with boundaries: learning to say no! There are a lot of benefits to learning how to verbalize your resistance to something. Firstly, it puts you in a better position to do what you want, then it allows you to create room for a much needed conversation about your needs, and finally, it helps you avoid any unnecessary commitments that might've been a burden to you.

In your workbook, you're going to answer the questions below as honestly and comprehensively as you can. Remember that no one is going to read your journal (always ensure that you put it in a safe place), so feel free to let it all out! The only rule here is that you're not allowed to overthink the process. In other words, there are no right or wrong answers unless you're trying to lie to yourself because you can't stand the thought of confronting the truth. Do not think about any grammar or spelling mistakes and feel free to go for as long as your mind allows you to.

While this exercise aims to teach you how to say no, it firstly addresses your level of self-awareness. That is, your conscious knowledge of your mental state, your emotions, and how they relate to your character and behavior.

1. For me, self-love is…
2. Looking back on your life and relationships, what kind of boundaries do you believe people have overstepped? (Do you feel forced to engage in activities? Or do you believe there is someone who always hurts your feelings the way they talk to you?)
3. Imagine the line that separates you from the rest of the world. If you're standing on the other side, what kind of space do you aspire to find yourself in? Try to cover the physical, financial, sexual, emotional, spiritual, and mental aspects of your life. Maybe you grew up in a family that followed a specific religion, now you just want to go out into the world and follow your spiritual path. Maybe you no longer want to feel judged by your family about the kind of relationship you have with your partner, or you simply wish your boss would stop talking to you so rudely or treating you so badly. Write them all down!
4. Think of four people in your life that you believe should get a lesson on how you should be treated. To make this exercise more effective, try to find one from different aspects of your life (maybe a colleague from work, a family member, a friend, and your partner). Then, describe your relationships with these individuals, paying special attention to the way they make you feel and how you feel about them. What kind of "no" would you like to apply in your relationships with these people and why?

From question four, you might've realized that not every no comes in the form of actually saying "no". For example, sometimes you don't mind assisting someone, you just wish they would communicate with you better. In another relationship, you might find that you're struggling to have your points respected, so you'd like to create an environment where you'll feel heard, and your views will be respected. That is understandable, so don't second guess yourself for feeling like that.

_____
_____
_____
_____
_____
_____
_____

The best way to ensure that your boundaries are taken seriously consider doing the following:

• Reiterate Your No

Your nagging sister comes to you again and asks for some money. Even though she promises to pay you back, you know she won't! The request is always urgent and no matter how much you try, you obviously can't find it in you to say no. What you should do in this instance is take a deep breath, close your eyes and blurt out the word "no." Simple! It's going to feel scary, your heart will pound violently, and you might even cry, but just do it and anticipate the silence. From there on, they might nag and try to soften you up with stories but what you need to do here is continue saying no, even if you're required to say it 1oo times. Shake your head or adjust your tone to make it firmer, but do not back down until they understand your answer.

- **Strategize Your Answer**

Maybe your sister pays you back, but you want to teach her that you're not always available to save her every time she pressures you. The next time she calls frantically, take a two-minute pause before telling her that you'll have to check your budget or that you can only send it after you buy your groceries, which is tomorrow evening. The trick here is not to lie but to honestly communicate that you also have urgent commitments that you need to attend to. They knew they were going to need money, why did they not call you sooner? Again, remain firm by sticking to your answer, even if you can sense the disappointment in their voice or body language.

- **Give a Reason…Only When It's Required**

If providing a reason is necessary, start by taking a nice short breath, pause, and then explain your answer with a maximum of three sentences. Your answer should make it clear that your decision is final. You can achieve this by being firm because the more you try to elaborate on your answer, the more you open up the floor for the other person to challenge your decision.

If you cannot give your sister any money, tell her that although you empathize with her, the money you have is meant to cover your groceries for the rest of the month. Don't offer to give her whatever is left or make a plan on her behalf. It's not your responsibility to do so and she should be able to learn that by now.

- **Allow People to React Negatively to the Boundary**

In case you did not know this, letting people down is a natural part of life. Self-advocacy leader Selena Rezvani reiterates the importance of anticipating negative reactions from people after you assert yourself. "People may feel negatively toward you when you assert your boundaries. Expect and anticipate their resistance—see it as part of the fabric of standing up for yourself, and not a sign that you did anything wrong." (Rezvani, 2021, para. 1o). If your sister hangs up abruptly or bangs the door on their way out, don't attempt to run after them or call them back. Give them the space to react and reflect on the situation at the end because in any case, they still need to think about and understand- why you had to make that decision.

1. Over the next month, you're going to dedicate a week to establishing a boundary with the people you've mentioned above. In this workbook, think about the effective steps that you're going to take to reach this point. Using the example above, you'll spend the first week focusing on your sister and learning to turn down the urge to give her money. You'll practice the no you're going to give, the reasons you might have to provide, and how you're going to handle her negative reactions should there be any. When she finally asks for the money, write down your encounter with her and what it has taught you. If she indeed decides to give you space for a few days, do not reach out to her. Instead, allow her to come back to you and that is only when you'll have a conversation with her, detailing a way forward that will work for the both of you.

Ever Heard of Self-Care?

Self-care is the fulfilling act of engaging in activities that promote your mental, emotional, and physical well-being. While it might seem like a simple concept, most of us rarely give ourselves the love and attention we need. We always have an excuse that justifies why we could not go to the dentist, why we're still not scheduling an appointment with a therapist, and why we're still not eating healthy!

The exercise below is going to encourage you to continue putting yourself first by focusing on the things that you can do for yourself without feeling guilty or expecting it from anyone.

Exercise 3: A Love Language as a Gift

In this exercise, we're going to use Gary Chapman's concept of the five love languages to put ourselves at the core forefront of expressing and receiving love. The golden rule here is to make it all about you! Try not to engage anyone in any of these exercises because the aim is to be content in your own company and what you can do for yourself.

Although we're encouraged to learn the five love languages to better understand when our loved ones are being appreciative, it's just as important to know what it is that we need to feel loved. Of course, at this point, you're the only one who knows the kind of tenderness you've been yearning for.

Every week, you're going to focus on one love language that is going to dominate your life. These love languages do not come in any priority, the aim is to give them attention whenever you're able to. Just ensure that you dedicate a minimum of five days to them.

In this workbook, you'll be required to take a "before" picture, coupled with a brief entry detailing how you're feeling, what your expectations are, and what you're looking forward to. After the activity, take an "after" picture that will also be accompanied by an entry taking you through the activity, how you felt, whether your expectations were met, and how you intend to continue with the activity if it worked for you.

Are you excited to give yourself some love?

1. Week 1: Physical Touch

This is often expressed when one feels lonely, lost, and in need of fleshly assurance. When it comes to self-care, you're going to pay special attention to how you treat yourself on a physical level. You will also engage in activities that promote your awareness of your body as well as cater to its needs.

From the list below, pick a minimum of three activities that will promote physical touch in your life. Feel free to try out all the ideas offered below, and if you can think of an activity that is not included in this list, then you're also more than welcome to try it out too.

- **Get a massage:** Why don't you go out for a 30-minute session that will ensure that your feel-good hormones are released from your body while you destress from anything that might've been overwhelming you? You don't even need to get a full body massage. Maybe you just feel like getting your feet rubbed or you want your head massaged; whatever works for you, just make sure you enjoy the session!
- **Run an evening hot bath:** After a long day, it's advisable to grab a glass of wine or some fruit, play some relaxing music, dim the lights, and indulge in a long warm bubble bath. During this time, make sure that you don't think of anything or anyone that might trigger you or make you feel anxious. The aim is to take at the moment, appreciate your body, and let your imagination wander off with nothing but great thoughts!
- **Get physically active:** This week, visit the gym, go out for a night of dancing or engage in a fun activity like hiking or water aerobics. The aim here is to allow your body to take advantage of its capabilities while you focus on nothing but the pleasure that comes with them.
- **Take care of your face, hands, hair, and other intricate body parts:** Get your toiletry bag and massage your face and body with essential moisturizers. Pay attention to every part that you hold and appreciate it for its various functionalities. When you brush your hair, do it with gentleness and ensure that you give it all the nutrients and cleanliness it needs.
- **Get a "cuddle couch":** Whenever you watch your favorite shows or read a book, you can indulge in this non-human

delicacy that will make you warm and comfortable. It will allow you to feel protected while also comforting you, especially if you're having a bad day.

2. Week 2: Quality Time

Here, you are more focused on some much needed "me" time! You are a lovable and valuable being whose presence is still needed on this earth. You won't know this unless you give yourself the attention that you've been giving so freely and generously to everyone else.

- **Take yourself out on a date:** Whether you plan to go to your favorite restaurant, watch a movie, or prefer packing up a nice basket for a picnic, it's about time you detach from the world for a few hours! During this time, ensure that you don't succumb to any distractions like attending to work emails or long phone calls with your best friends. You're supposed to take this moment in by ordering your favorite food and drinks and reflecting on your life and the plans you'd like to pursue soon.
- **Find a balance between your personal and work life:** Aren't we all guilty of bringing some work home? It's an unhealthy habit that does not allow you to focus on your personal life. From now on, switch off all work notifications and avoid speaking about what you need to do at work as soon as you get home. There is nothing as important as having a meaningful life that does not involve your professional commitments. The more you do this, the more productive you'll be at work because you would've given yourself the time needed to refresh and energize yourself for work.
- **Read a book:** Reading is a healthy habit that not only empowers you with information but can also entertain you if you're more interested in fictional work. Why don't you head over to the bookstore and pick a book that interests you? Then,

commit to reading a few pages each day until you finish your good read.

- **RSVP:** How many times have you turned down invites simply because you believed you were too busy or had some excuses that prevented you from connecting with your loved ones? If you've been recently invited to something—even if it's as small as a coffee date—do yourself the favor and show up! No excuses, no overthinking it, and definitely no skipping even if you don't want to go

- **Cook your favorite meal:** For once, let it be just you, your ingredients, and a powerful recipe in the kitchen! It's time you cooked your favorite meal all on your own. To make this more fun, you can record yourself doing it and take your imaginary crowd on a fun adventure of transforming your favorite recipe into a good dish.

3. Week 3: Gifts

This language is all about rewarding yourself with gifts that are meaningful, inexpensive, and validate

- **Buy yourself an outfit or a home item:** You know that dress you've always had on your wish list? Now is the time to get it; you deserve it! Oftentimes, we discourage ourselves from getting new stuff because we convince ourselves we're too broke to splurge on unnecessary things. However, that can never be true! Think about all the things you conquered for the past 12 months and then tell yourself that you deserve to appreciate yourself by buying yourself something new. That good feeling you'll get once you bring your item home will be worth it!

- **Invest in your memories:** Forget your digital spaces. How about you dedicate some time to re-arranging your album or investing in a new one? Print out your special pictures and have them placed safely in your album. Write notes, reflect on the photos, and thank the higher powers for allowing you to cross paths with the people that you hold so close to your heart. your presence and efforts.

- **Use your talents:** We're all born with a talent that we've used to bless the people around us. How about we start spoiling ourselves with our gifts? If you're a singer and songwriter, write yourself a song and record it. If you're a poet, grab a pen and paper and let it all flow. Just do it! Everyone else has benefited from your gift; now it's your turn to experience it all.

- **Give someone you love something:** Yes, I did say these exercises should be solely focused on you, but there is power in doing something for someone. Nursing Director at Behavioral Health Services Kitty Stafford agrees. "Your brain's pleasure circuits are stimulated by acts of charity and release 'good feeling' chemicals such as endorphins, which give you a sense of euphoria, and oxytocin, which promotes tranquility and inner peace." (2016, para. 6).

- **Get yourself flowers:** Do you even know what your favorite flowers are? You have so many reasons to invest in a colorful and meaningful bouquet this week! Go to a florist, pick your flowers, and smile all the way home!

4. Week 4: Acts of Service

Sometimes you feel drained and too overwhelmed. You need this love language to experience thoughtful gestures that ensure that you feel important and wanted. While you might think it's almost impossible to give yourself acts of service as you don't have the time or energy- to commit to such, it's easier than you think to express this love language for yourself.

- **Order in:** For just a day, focus on all things except cooking! We all know that figuring out what you're going to eat for supper can be quite a mission, let alone having to prepare it yourself. For this exercise, just go to your favorite delivery app or website and order the healthiest and tastiest meat that you and your family will enjoy. The best part about this is that you won't have to worry about washing the dishes afterward!

- **Accept help:** The reason we feel overwhelmed at times is that our pride does not allow us to get the help we need. The next time your mom or best friend offers to babysit your kids for the weekend, take up the offer without feeling any guilt. They're doing it because they love you and can see that you need help. It has nothing to do with you being weak or incompetent. You'll notice the difference it's going to make in your life.

- **Ask for help:** Yes, or speak up if you feel like you've been given too much responsibility. This happens especially at work when your manager feels like you're the only person capable of doing things that are outside of your job spec. The next time they hand you another project, decline politely by letting them know that you're still busy with the other project before suggesting that another person should do it. If this happens more at home, consider delegating some tasks to your partner or your children.

- **Declutter your space:** It's a real act of self-love. Put on your headphones, play your favorite music and tidy up your bedroom or do your laundry. Not only will you end up with a cleaner space, but you'll feel good about having something clean to wear or sleeping in a neater space.

- **Get organized:** Make your life easier by getting into the habit of planning. This will reduce your stress levels and allow you to relax a little more. Have a to-do list that helps you get all the important things, like paying your bills or attending to certain tasks done every day. The more you do this, the more you'll feel like you're accomplishing more in life. This is something that has always been true, you've just been neglecting to acknowledge it.

5. **Week 5: Words of Affirmation**

In case you didn't know this, your inner self still needs to hear from you that you're a blessing to have in this lifetime. For this love language, you're going to use genuine and meaningful words to express this.

- **Write a letter to yourself:** Every month, write a letter to yourself. Thank yourself for having the courage to conquer certain obstacles, encourage yourself to accomplish certain goals, and reflect on the lessons you keep on learning. This cultivates a meaningful relationship with yourself and enables you to value your growth and transformation. After a year, dedicate some time to reading the letters you've been writing to yourself, and you'll be blown away by the level of wisdom you possess.

- **Write a letter to someone you love:** Again, this is a selfless act that will make you feel good. Whether you'll give them the letter or not is up to you, but just think of 12 people that you admire and believe should know just how important they are to you. Then, every month, write a letter to them telling them how much you appreciate them and why you're thankful for their presence in your life.

- **Leave yourself a note:** Get sticky notes that you can in random places in your house. Then, write yourself a fun note that will encourage you to keep going, even on your worst days. What is your favorite quote? What do you love the most about yourself? What does your inner self need to know? Write them all down and read them every time you bump into them; they will uplift your mood!

- **Focus on your strengths:** What are you good at and what should you start doing more about it? So many times, we like to talk ourselves down by focusing on our weaknesses and shortcomings, which is so demoralizing. Every morning, for about a month, start verbalizing the one thing you're grateful for being good at. Verbalize it with confidence and think about it for the rest of the day. After a month, you'll notice that saying these powerful words each morning allows you to have a more productive day, no matter how many things go wrong.

- **Forgive yourself:** For 12 weeks, think about 12 things that you need to forgive yourself for. These can be recent things or stuff you got involved in during your school days. This exercise is all about learning to be gentle with yourself so you're going to tell your younger or immature self why you've chosen to forgive them, the lessons you learned, and why you believe your mistakes helped you to become a better person today. This is the most powerful thing you can learn to do for yourself.

Exercise 4: Self-Care Vision Board

Do you know how we're always encouraged to create a vision board that indicates the things we'd like to manifest in our lives? This large, colorful, and creative poster requires you to paste quotes that motivate you, materialistic items you'd like to acquire, places you'd like to go to, and the direction you'd like your career to take.

In this exercise, you're going to do exactly that, but your board will be entirely focused on self-care. This means anything you put into the board will include quotes that you live by that encourage you to take care of yourself better. Pictures that indicate what self-care looks like for you. Do you envision yourself getting a massage at a spa? Are you reading a book? Or is the first thing that comes to mind a powerful picture of a woman taking a nap? Whatever it is, you're going to add it to your board!

For this exercise you'll need:

- an A3 board
- A3 blank paper
- magazines, books, and newspapers
- scissors24
- stickers, decorations, glitter
- markers, crayons, pencils
- white craft or PVA paper glue/adhesive
- your laptop, computer or smartphone
- a printing machine
- about 2 hours of your time

Steps:

1. Use either your laptop or magazines to gather pictures, quotes, or affirmations that will encourage you to prioritize self-care. Most of the pictures on the board should include the kind of things you haven't tried in your life but look forward to participating in, soon. (Maybe you want to go hiking? Have

always wanted to try a hot stone massage? Or would like to visit your favorite restaurant alone and order every meal that appeals to you?

2. Then arrange and stick your pictures on your vision board. Be creative—let it be loud, daring, and motivational. Believe it or not, one day you're going to let it all out!

3. After you've arranged your artwork, stick it up where you'll see it every day. Maybe on your bedroom wall or somewhere in your living room.

4. Every time you come across your self-care vision board, analyze it, take in the emotions each picture or quote elicits, and allow your mind to convince you that this should be your reality!

Although we're often told that vision boards attract the things we specified in our boards to manifest into reality, we still have a responsibility to ensure that they indeed happen. You might have a picture of a woman taking a peaceful nap on your board, tell yourself that you're going to do just that before the end of the month. Then, do it! Clear your diary, submit any outstanding work on time, send your children to their grandparents for a weekend (or a night) then take a long warm bath-which should also be on your vision board-and then sleep! Sometimes it is that simple.

_____

_____

_____

_____

_____

_____

_____

_____

_____

_____

Chasing Purposeful Living

Author and Entrepreneur Meghan French Dunbar say a purposeful life is "using your unique gifts to make consistent contributions toward a worthy cause(s) while intentionally building a life that you love." (n.d., para 2). When breaking this down, you get the idea that to serve yourself, you need to be cognizant of your unique gifts, and worthy causes that you want to engage in, and intentionally build the life of your dreams. This is the only way you can achieve true happiness and won't get drained, even if you're helping people. Furthermore, it will boost your self-esteem as you'll have a greater appreciation of yourself.

Exercise 5: Connecting With a Higher Purpose

For the next two weeks, focus on the three important elements that make up a purposeful life. You must spend nothing more than two weeks to get your answers, as it can be quite tempting to relax and ultimately end up neglecting these important questions. Using this workbook, answer the questions below.

1. What are my top five unique gifts?
2. What are worthy causes that I want to contribute to?

3. How am I going to intentionally build a life that I know I'll love?

For the third question, ensure that you break down your goals by focusing on short-term ones that you can start implementing now, and establishing long-term inspirations that you envision for yourself. Dare yourself to go back to school, tackle a habit like smoking, or fix relationships with people that you still need in your life.

CHAPTER 2: A Look Into Self-Esteem

You yourself, as much as anybody in the entire universe, deserve your love and affection.

- Sharon Salzberg

Self-esteem and self-love go hand in hand. This is because, in its simplest form, self-esteem is defined as an individual's "overall subjective sense of personal worth or value. In other words, self-esteem may be defined as how much you appreciate and like yourself, regardless of the circumstances." (Cherry, 2021, para. 3). When you have low self-esteem, you often find yourself being shameful and in despair. Once you're able to achieve a healthy level of self-esteem you will be able to appreciate your most authentic form.

Why Do People Struggle With Self-Esteem?

The reasons are unique to every individual, but the common denominators are often stressful life events, sudden changes, the loss of loved ones, and illnesses. In essence, when an individual feels like they're too overwhelmed with everything going on around them, their confidence takes a dip. What might make matters worse is when they believe they've failed way too many times to consider themselves capable of taking control of their lives.

How to Achieve Good Self-Esteem

In this chapter, we're going to focus on an exciting way to build your self-esteem without having to overthink its practicalities of it. You see, self-esteem is something that comes from the inside and is ultimately reflected externally. In the previous, you learned how to be assertive by establishing boundaries. While you won't instantly recognize how it builds your self-esteem, the way you carry yourself, react to individual relationships that you have with your loved ones, and approach life will gradually take a positive turn. Now that you've learned to appreciate yourself a little better by putting yourself first, it's time to raise yourself by challenging yourself to grow.

Exercise 6: Challenge Yourself

Step 1: Identify Your Beliefs

List five negative beliefs that you have about yourself. Remember that with self-esteem, your beliefs are not necessarily facts but are personal opinions that you adopted over time as you grew up. The aim here is to investigate whether you're being objective or subjective in your personal views. When writing down your beliefs, ensure that you write them in the first person and that you spread them across the various aspects of your life. Additionally, consider giving examples to solidify your claims. For example, you might write down:

- I believe I am fat. Growing up, I was the biggest of all my siblings. This resulted in my friends and family calling me "fatty." This is a statement that has followed me throughout my life. I watch what I wear, I have an unhealthy relationship with food, and I am conscious of my body, especially in public settings.

- I don't think I am smart. I've always been an average student, and I failed to get enrolled in the university of my dreams. Even as a career woman, I don't think I have what it takes to make it to the top.

- I don't make a great partner. Looking back on my relationships, I've never really managed to make things work. My relationships always end with my partner leaving me in the most hurtful way.

The examples above looked at three different aspects of a person's life. They have a statement (or belief), an explanation of where the belief comes from, and how it has affected the person's self-esteem or outlook towards life. Now it's time to write down yours.

Step 2: Formulate a Plan

Now comes the interesting part! After stating your beliefs, you'll notice that you somehow managed to dilute facts with opinions. Unsurprisingly, you'll also notice that you have the power to change this outlook because you were able to identify the root cause of the belief. It is now your responsibility to challenge yourself to do something about these beliefs so that you may formulate positive beliefs about yourself. Looking at the examples above, we can come up with the following solutions:

- In terms of body image, find out what the healthiest weight should be for a person of your height and age. Then, challenge yourself to do something about it if you're indeed overweight or justified in aspiring for a specific weight. Once you've done this, you'll now have to think of practical ways to adjust your lifestyle. What changes are you going to make to your diet? Are you going to join a gym? And how will you ensure that you start dressing up appropriately and comfortably for your body?

- Looking at the second issue, how about you enroll in a short-term course that will help you upskill yourself? You don't have to be a genius to successfully pass a six-week course, especially if you're going to be focused and dedicated to ensuring that you make the most of it. Go online and try out a free class that will help you obtain a skill you've always wanted to try out. Maybe school might not be an ideal option at the moment, but don't despair! If you're more concerned about career growth, speak to your Human Resources Department and find out if there are any mentorship or job shadowing programs that they support. From there, you'll be able to identify someone or a department that you're interested in that can help you grow professionally. There will be no pressure on you to be a genius, either. You'll walk into that space knowing that you're more interested in learning than proving that you know the work.

You never know how taking a chance like this can change your career!

- Finally, if you believe you're destined to attract frogs in the relationship department, then start re-evaluating the reasons why you might find people running away from you or why you should raise your standards to attract people who will value you as the special and unique individual that you are. Do you communicate your insecurities excessively when in a relationship? Do you find yourself ignoring red flags simply because you don't want to want to be lonely? Investigate the reasons why your relationships have failed before by focusing on the things that you can control. If your ex left because even when you gave it your all, then move right along with the belief that the right person will come at the right time. As cliched as this might sound, it is true!

Step 3: Set Yourself up for Success

Have you ever wondered why it's so easy for some people to reach their goals? No matter how difficult things get for them, if they set certain goals for themselves, they're guaranteed to achieve all they aspire for! To be honest, none of these people operates on luck or the right connections, nor are they overconfident or justifiably arrogant. They have simply learned how to set themselves up for success by following a compelling formula that guarantees them success all the time. The best part about this formula is that the more they manage to achieve their goals, the higher their self-esteem goes, making it even easier for them to achieve the next goal!

To join this elite group of successful individuals, you can follow an approach known as the "SMART goal" tool. This plan follows the acronym that stands for specific, measurable, achievable, realistic, and timely. After establishing the five challenges you're going to engage in, use the tool below to ensure that you succeed.

Specific: Every time you set a goal for yourself, ensure that you know what exactly it is that you're trying to achieve. It's clear that you'd like to lose weight, but how much? Of course, you want career growth, but what does that mean for you and the industry that you work in? Do not shy away from giving as many valuable details as possible.

Measurable: For every goal, you should be able to have a criterion that allows you to track your progress. This is an important aspect that lets you determine whether there are any urgent changes that you need to make to your goal or if you should pat yourself on the back for making courageous progress. Let's say you've given yourself five months to drop a jean size and transition into a healthier lifestyle. Within these five months, you'll want to ensure that you eliminate junk food from your diet by month one, that you go to the gym every week by the second month, and that you start drinking eight glasses of water each day by the third month. If you don't meet up to these expectations, then you've got to hold yourself accountable.

Achievable: The reason why you're witnessing the same people reaching their goals all the time it's because they go for things that they know are possible to achieve! Of course, you're more than capable of achieving a lot in your life, but you've got to be realistic about what you can and can't do at the moment. You can't aspire to have a million dollars in your bank account if you've got a debt to clear and still working in a junior position in your company. However, you might aspire for financial freedom, which means clearing your debt, getting a side hustle, and saving a considerable amount of money monthly. Do you notice the difference between those two sentences?

Realistic: Although this might sound identical to achievable, realistic goals are centered around chasing things that are within reach and are relevant to your life. In other words, your goals should align with who you are, what you believe in, and where you see yourself in the long term. Instead of aspiring to shadow your CEO at work, wouldn't it make sense for you to work on the skills needed in your current job role to build your credibility and get the recognition you deserve?

Instead of just aspiring to be rich so that you can afford all the flashiest and fastest cars, shouldn't you rather focus on being financially stable enough to take care of yourself and your family?

Timely: This step is important, as it will enable you to realize the sense of urgency around your matter. How many times have you set goals for yourself and ended up giving up on them simply because you believe there's still time to pursue them again? Your expected victory date should be realistic, ambitious, and allow you to navigate what should take priority when chasing your goal. Do not put too much pressure on yourself by picking a date that is too soon and certainly refrain from giving yourself a year to achieve your goals. The time is now, and you can make it!

Exercise 7: Learning to Acknowledge Your Successes

The final step to building your self-esteem requires you to reflect on your life and acknowledge how powerful you are! Imagine the obstacles, pitfalls, and challenges you've overcome to get this far! Unfortunately, you've allowed certain factors in your life to affect your ability to appreciate yourself and remain strong, even when you feel like you're destined to fail.

I cannot stress how important this exercise is! Not only does it eliminate the negative things you've been highlighting about yourself, but it also has the power to energize you, especially on your worst days. From this evening, you're going to reflect on just one thing that you accomplished in your life. Start from your childhood years and think about the proud moments that you had that some people might not even know about. Write down:

- What it is that you accomplished.
- Why it makes you proud to have achieved your goal or conquered an obstacle.
- An important lesson you learned and how you can use it to make better decisions in your life.

Be careful not to downplay your achievements by using harmful words such as "it's not a big deal" "anyone could've done it" or "I got lucky". If your accomplishments could elicit some positive emotions back then, then it means they are still valid.

On some evenings, you'll struggle to think of things that happened way back, and that's completely okay. When that happens, think about the day you had and reflect on one good thing you're proud of accomplishing. The more you engage in this exercise, the more you'll realize that there's just so much to be proud of. There are days when you'll feel like you don't have what it takes to get out of bed and show up at work. A few hours later, you'll be back home and wondering where did you get the strength to make it? Do you know what is the first thing you should do? Acknowledge that you made it out of bed and successfully had a productive day at work. That's more than an accomplishment and you should take pride in it!

This is not an exercise that you should do for a specific time only, it's one that I'd recommend you incorporate into your lifestyle. Do it daily! On some evenings, you won't have the stamina to write down your successes. That's also fine! If your heart tells you to reflect while you're bathing, when you're doing the dishes, or just before you sleep, then allow yourself to. The most important part here is that you acknowledge how great you are!

Exercise 8: It's Time to Get Into Character!

This is going to be a fun one! It is mainly based on how we're so quick to identify the things we admire about people but fail to notice similar or stronger traits that we possess as well. It's about learning to capitalize on these strengths by being bold enough to invest in a transformation.

Do you remember the time Beyoncé released an album titled Sasha Fierce? During that time, she almost brought the world to a standstill when she revealed that Sasha Fierce is her alter ego who helps her manage her jitters whenever she hits the stage. "She doesn't do interviews, she only performs. It's kind of like doing a movie. When you put on the wig and put on clothes, you walk differently. It's no different from anyone else. I feel like we all kind of have that thing that takes over." (Stallings, 2022, para. 3).

So, the songstress realized she had a problem of getting super nervous whenever she had to hit the stage. She realized that she could not allow this to get the better of her because it would ruin her career. Instead of having a prolonged pity party about it, the star decided to come up with a plan that would ensure that she deals with it internally, while also continuing to deliver the quality work that she's known for.

Like Beyoncé, I want you to adopt an alter ego that is going to enable you to tap into your inner power. Your alter ego does not necessarily have to cause a dramatic change in your persona, but it should be able to bring about the desired change that's necessary to raise your self-esteem.

One of the best ways to achieve this is by looking at someone that inspires you. It could be your mom, your aunt, or even a celebrity that you've always admired. Without overthinking it, think of an individual in your life that you believe has good self-esteem. Then:

1. Name three top character traits that you believe they possess. These are traits that you know you lack and would like to develop to feel good about yourself. Are they confident? Do you wish you were just as assertive as they are? Or do you wish you could speak your mind just like they always do?

2. Then, write down how they exude these beautiful character traits. In other words, maybe you want to adopt your sister's assertiveness. You want to be able to speak your mind and be heard, have the power to say no without feeling guilty, and draw healthy boundaries so that people find it easier to respect the decisions you make in your life.

3. In this step, I need you to write down how you're going to fit their character traits into yours. Remember, you're not trying to compare yourself to your sister or be like her; you just want to have what she has. If, for example, you're having issues with your body image and admire how your aunt always can dress well for her body even though she's not a model, then you're going to note that she dresses well for her body, meaning you need to start doing the same on your side. It's also important that you observe and note down their body language. How does your sister ensure that people respect her no? Are you looking into using your hands during communication just like your favorite motivational speaker does simply because you noticed how it gets people to pay attention for longer? This is your time to develop a powerful character!

4. After you've written down the changes you want to make in your life, strategize a compelling plan that will ensure you execute it as best as you can. Now that you know you need to start dressing for your body type, when are you going to go out for some fun shopping? If you're inspired by your mom's ability to go back to school even when the odds were stacked against her, then think about how you can make that possible for yourself, too. Find a good school and course to study, get started on your application, ask your HR department if they

offer bursaries, or find alternative funding solutions that will suit your needs.

5. If you want to enjoy the effectiveness of this exercise, do not tell anyone about it. Just wake up every morning telling yourself that you're stepping into a specific alter ego or individual. Walk like them, talk like them, take yourself out on a solo lunch, and when the waiter approaches you, get into character and watch your confidence get a much needed boost! The best part about it is that the people around you are going to notice it, too. When they ask, laugh it off and answer confidently that you're working on yourself and having a great time. No matter how weird it will feel initially, you're going to get used to it and thank yourself for taking the chance.

After a month of embodying someone, reflect on:

- how you felt the first time you had to step into their character.
- how you felt when someone reacted positively to your behavior (especially the person you're emulating, if they're around your circle).
- what you enjoyed the most about this exercise.
- how you'll ensure you continue executing these character traits.

A few years after Beyoncé introduced us to Sasha Fierce, she shocked us again when she announced that she no longer relies on her alter ego to overcome the stage jitters. "I killed her. I don't need Sasha Fierce anymore, because I've grown and now, I'm able to merge the two" (Crosley, 2010, para. 3). No! I'm not insisting that you should go and kill your aunt in a few years, but I'm telling you this because I want you to realize that once you tap into your power, you'll no longer feel the need to hide behind an alter ego. The more you practice embodying characteristics that you admire, the easier it'll be for them to form part of your personality, attitude, and behavior!

CHAPTER 3: Practicing Compassion... on Yourself!

Remember, you have been criticizing yourself for years and it hasn't worked. Try approving of yourself and see what happens.

- Louise L. Hay

Lea Seigen Shinraku, a therapist, writer, and long-time meditator experienced the power of self-compassion when she was driving home from school one evening. It seemed as if the saga started of nowhere! Her car started overheating shortly before her engine gave up on her.

Now, stuck in the middle of the road, causing a traffic buildup and having her anxiety increased by cars speeding off and occasionally beeping out of anger, Shinraku could not help but start blaming herself for this embarrassing inconvenience. "Why didn't I notice earlier that the car was overheating? I should have had it serviced. If I had been more on top of things, this wouldn't be happening." (Shinraku, 2013, para. 5). Of course, she tried to maintain control of the situation by calling for help. She was told that a tow truck would arrive within 30 minutes, and to be honest, this did not calm her down or cause her to be any gentler with herself.

"I'm in the way; inconveniencing everyone around me. I'm taking up too much space." (Shinraku, 2013, para. 7). It was during this abusive state of mind that a passenger knocked on her window. Not another driver trying to make her feel more guilty than she already is! Out of reluctance and a little bit of shame, Shinraku lowered her window to give him a chance.

The guy smiled, greeted politely, and told her he worked at the cafe not far from where she was stuck. Courteously, he asked if she wanted

"A latte or a chai or something," (Shinraku, 2013, para. 9). Startled by this guy's kindness, she responded by saying she'd like chamomile tea.

For a minute, the self-blaming and criticizing paused. Shinraku wondered why this guy was being so nice to her when this was somehow her fault. Why is he even offering her something to drink when everyone else has been so hard on her? Before she could even attempt to come up with an answer, the guy was back again, this time holding the hot beverage that she asked for.

She thanked him, and just as she was about to pay him, he smiled again, and said, "Oh, no, don't worry about it... Hey, I've been there." (Shinraku, 2013, para. 26). The sweet samaritan closed off this unbelievable scene by tapping twice on her window before disappearing back into this hostile reality. It was at this moment that Shinraku realized that actually, this wasn't her fault! Something unfortunate happened to her, and she had no way of predicting that it was going to happen. Furthermore, it was during this dramatic moment that she had to be much gentler with herself, just as the stranger was.

I know without a doubt that you can somehow relate to this story. There are a lot of instances where you blamed yourself for things you could not control, treated yourself with hostility, and probably still struggle to forgive yourself for some mistakes you did too. It's something that happens a lot, but that does not mean it's natural or acceptable; it's some form of self-loathing that is unhealthy and dangerous.

In its simplest form, self-compassion is not self-pity or selfishness; it will not affect your potential to grow and succeed, and it does not make you overly sensitive. It is expressing concern for unfortunate circumstances and going out of your way to relieve the mental, emotional, and physical pains experienced during the difficult time. Using this definition, does it not scare you how we're always willing and ready to show others compassion and neglect to do it for ourselves? Shinraku is the perfect example of this! She decided to criticize herself during a challenging time while a total stranger offered to show her kindness.

How about you start practicing powerful exercises that empower you to stop being so hard on yourself? If another stranger can notice that you need more love and gentleness, then it's only fair that you treat yourself with the same level of kindness!

Exercise 9: Forgive Yourself

You don't know how to be good to yourself because you're still holding on to things that should not even be a continued problem in your life.

Unforgiveness is a dangerous thing to have in your life, especially if you're directing it toward yourself. To make this exercise effective, you are going to use the purest definition of forgiveness to understand why you should confront your mistakes or regrets. Kendra Cherry, an author and educator, uses the perfect definition: she writes that forgiveness is "a deliberate decision to let go of feelings of anger, resentment, and retribution toward someone who you believe has wronged you." (2021, para. 1). When directing it to yourself, you can understand that you need to be willing to let go of all these negative emotions that you've brought onto yourself by ruminating over past events.

Self-forgiveness requires you to focus on the four Rs that complete this necessary act:

1. Responsibility: This involves facing what has happened so that you can accept your reality.
2. Remorse: It's okay to feel guilty after experiencing something unpleasant. This triggers you to aspire for positive behavior as opposed to feeling shameful and worthless.
3. Restoration: This requires you to think about repairing any damages that might have been brought on by the mistake and

looking for effective ways to restore trust, especially within yourself.

4. Renewal: Now that you've acknowledged your mistakes, it's time to focus on moving on by identifying compelling methods that will prevent you from repeating the same mistakes. One way to achieve this is by asking yourself what it is that tempted you to behave the way that you did.

Now, you are going to use the information above to write a letter to yourself. Think about a mistake, an incident you regret, or a decision you made a long time ago that still haunts you today. This should be something that has prevented you from living your life joyously or trusting yourself with important decisions. It should be an event that has elicited nothing but negative emotions and even caused you to think negatively about yourself. Writing this letter to yourself means you are ready to let go of this mistake and ready to embrace a guilt-free future.

If you're still reluctant to grab your pen and get started, consider the benefits below:

- It raises your level of self-awareness: This means that you will walk away feeling empowered because you'll have an improved ability to observe your thoughts, actions, and emotions objectively. It helps you understand why you should continue doing something things and why now is the right time to re-evaluate some values that have been governing your life. There is no doubt that this will be uncomfortable, emotionally taxing, and may be upsetting, but you can only grow if you're comfortable with the truth that you know about yourself.

- You'll perceive time differently: Author Erin Falconer once wrote a letter to her future self while she was in high school. Her English teacher, who proposed this exercise to her students, promised that she'd mail the letters back to her students in five years, just as they would be ready to graduate from college. Falconer did not understand this exercise but took part in it anyway, and she'll never forget her reaction when she got to read it again years after she wrote it several years ago. "I will never forget reading that letter when it came back to me, exactly five years later, as she had promised. It was a rare chance to reflect honestly on the passage of time and my personal growth over that formative period in my life. When I opened my letter, I was blown away by two things—how much I had changed, and how little I had changed." (Falconer, 2015, para. 10). Although you'll be reflecting on the past rather than anticipating the future, this exercise will still prove to you that you're an amazing individual who evolving continuously in the most positive way.

- Promotes healing: There is power in expressing yourself and reclaiming your power through the useful vigor of words. Holding a grudge only makes you unhappy and unproductive, but setting your intentions with words triggers you to do something about what you've written. You'll find yourself pursuing healing, working hard to let go, and learning to be gentler with yourself.

Pick a date and place where you know you'll experience little to no destruction. It can be in your backyard, your bedroom, or at the office after hours. Then:

1. Start writing about the incident that you want to forgive yourself for. Be honest, state your emotions, but most importantly, start by establishing an intention. What is it that you'd like to achieve by writing this letter? Is it forgiveness? Clarity? Or the ability to acknowledge your emotions?

2. Use the four Rs to break down your story. What are you taking responsibility for? Why are you feeling so guilty? How would you like to claim restoration? And how does renewal look and feel for you?

3. Remember, you're writing a letter to your younger self; why do you believe she deserves forgiveness so much?
4. Tell your younger self that you love her. Repeat it as many times as you have to.
5. Focus on the lessons your younger self has taught you that you appreciate so much.
6. Explain to your younger self why she deserves to be treated with kindness and gentleness.
7. How are you going to ensure that you introduce kindness and gentleness into your life?

After writing this letter, allow yourself to breathe and take in all the emotions that you're feeling at that moment. Embrace them and continue to tell your younger self that it will all be okay as you're about to close the chapter on this incident.

Some people struggle to decide what to do with their letters. For some, keeping it in their space opens up the opportunity to continue being shameful. Others want to keep it and read it after a while simply because they want to remind themselves of the final paragraphs that give them a renewed sense of hope. It's entirely up to you; do what makes you comfortable.

If you decide to dispose of it, make it clear that you're only doing it because you are willing to let go and focus on a new chapter in your life. If you decide to keep it, ensure that you keep it in a safe place where it will be out of reach from people who might be tempted to read it. Finally, there is another option that might work for you: tear off the part that speaks about the incident and keep the paragraphs that give you hope and make you fall in love with yourself all over again!

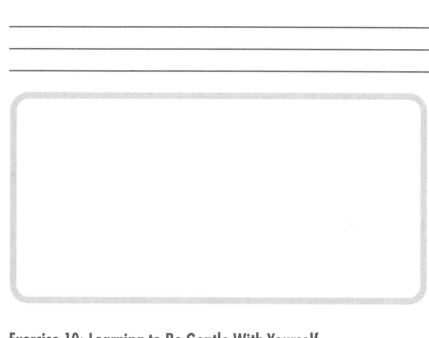

Exercise 10: Learning to Be Gentle With Yourself

Now that you've learned to forgive yourself, you need to start thinking of practical ways that will enable you to treat yourself with kindness. Below are tips you should incorporate into your life, especially to alter your choice of words, your actions, and the thoughts that you entertain.

1. Apologize when you use harmful words on yourself.

   Write down ten harmful words that you use daily. This includes words or sentences like "I'm stupid," "ugly," "failure," or any sentence that starts with "I should be..." "I could be..." or "I should've..."

   Every time you use these words throughout the day, pause, take a deep breath, and apologize to yourself for being so heartless and insulting. Say your apologies with conviction and ensure that you explain to yourself that you're learning how to be gentle with the amazing being that you are. For example, if you say something negative about your physical appearance, you can stop and say, "Girl, I'm so sorry for calling you ugly. Have you seen how gorgeous your eyes are? Relax, you're only learning how to be gentle with yourself. You're a work in progress and we'll get there soon." Simple, effective, and it will boost your mood and self-esteem!

2. Take in a compliment.

   Just because you're struggling to appreciate yourself doesn't mean you should block others from acknowledging how invaluable you are! The next time someone compliments you, pay special attention to the way you respond. There is no need to brush it off with an awkward sentence that downplays what the other person is saying or stops people from highlighting positive things about you! Practice smiling and just say thank you. That is all! It won't feel natural the first few times, but after a while, not only will the sentence come out more organically, but you will begin to believe the beautiful things that are being said about you.

3. Acknowledge a moment of suffering.

   Listen, suffering is a natural part of life! You're going to lose loved ones, deal with challenging situations, get your heart broken, and wonder why you walk around with such bad luck! Every single person you know-even the most famous people-go through moments of suffering. It does not matter how big or small your suffering is, but you need to learn how to acknowledge them. The best way to do this is to verbalize it when you find yourself going through it. Whether you're crying yourself to sleep or stuck in traffic just like Shinraku, you need to learn how to pause and say, "This is a moment of suffering and it's not my fault." It's never your fault! Mistakes happen, people betray us, we ignore red flags, and we act too hastily, but blaming yourself is the last thing you should do.

   The second part of this tip requires you to understand that compassion involves expressing concern over the misfortunes of others and in this case, yourself. Of course, you won't get out of your car and walk to a coffee shop while trying to deal with a stuck car that's causing traffic! However, you can take in a deep breath, ignore the rude comments and actions that others project toward you, and help yourself by calling for or accepting some assistance. In any moment of suffering, ask yourself, *What can I do to help myself physically, emotionally, or mentally?*

4. Confront your inner critic.

Do you know that loud, brutal, and annoying voice that always speaks down to you? Yes, the one you always believe whenever it has something distasteful to say about you. You need to learn how to shut it down! Even when your heart is beating fast and your voice trembles, establish a firm and bold tone that can shut it off instantly. The minute you hear your voice telling you that you're stupid, that you should've done or said something instead, close your heads, count to three and exclaim courageously, "Shut up! That is not true, and you know it!" Or belittle it by saying, "Oh, the inner critic, of course, it's you again. What pathetic thing have you got for me to ignore?" Again, you're going to feel crazy for establishing such methods, but they work! You just need to give them enough practice to experience their power!

To be better prepared for such instances, revisit the harmful words and statements you identified in the first point. Then, change those words and statements to formulate positive and uplifting sentences that you can use every time your inner voice tempts you with those old, boring ones that you've gotten used to! If your inner critic tells you that "you're too stupid to get a promotion or complete a project," respond by saying, "If I were stupid, I would not be here. I would've never been employed this long, and I would've never submitted my last project." Challenge it with facts, because that's what we operate on!

5. State your intentions every morning.

   Identify one way you're going to exercise gentleness on yourself each morning. Don't just state your intention but go out there and ensure that you do it! If you want to get a break sometime during the day, tell yourself that you're going to use your lunch hour to enjoy your food outside of your working space. If you want to improve your health by drinking more water, then state it in the morning! Say, "Today I intend to drink eight glasses of water, because I care for my health, and I appreciate the benefits." If you do this for the next 12 months, you'll wake up one day having been intentionally good to yourself a minimum of 365 days in a year. How powerful is that?

Exercise 11: Negative Distortions

To silence our inner critics and challenge the negative self-talk that haunts us daily, we need to understand what brought them into our lives or mentalities in the first place.

Cognitive distortions are biased perspectives we take on ourselves and the world around us. They are irrational thoughts and beliefs that we unknowingly reinforce over time. (Ackerman, 2017, para. 9). These thoughts are dangerous, as they are false and inaccurate, cause you to operate on a disruptive cycle of thinking, and lead to psychological damage.

In this exercise, you're going to do an honest introspection of the kind of negative self-talk and thinking that you're struggling with. You're going to identify the kind of distortion, expand more on it, and adopt new ways of thinking that will make you realize you've been lying and being too hard on yourself.

Steps:

1. There are eleven distortions listed below. Familiarize yourself with the titles and definitions and then decide on which one you relate to more.

All-or-Nothing Thinking: People with this type of thinking see things in terms of extremes. It's either something amazing or it's the worst thing ever. Because of this type of thinking, they also believe that they're either perfect individuals or failures that have no chance of making anything a success.

Personalization: This involves taking things personally or blaming yourself for things or situations even though you cannot provide any logical reasons why you should be to blame. For example, you could go out for lunch with a group of loved ones and come back home convinced that you're the reason why one of your cousins was being moody throughout the social gathering.

Fortune Telling: Distorted fortune tellers take in little to no evidence to create predictions or conclusions that are often unreasonable. Do you believe your marriage is destined to fail simply because your mother and sister walked away from their marriages? Do you believe you'll never get a promotion because you did not go to a certain school?

Discounting the Positive: Also known as the mental filter, this thinking disregards all the positives and causes you to focus on one single negative event that overshadows all the other ones. "An example of this distortion is one partner in a romantic relationship dwelling on a single negative comment made by the other partner and viewing the relationship as hopelessly lost, while ignoring the years of positive comments and experiences." (Ackerman, 2017, para. 18).

Disqualifying the positive: Maybe you don't necessarily filter out any positive things, but you disregard the positive ones that you have going on. When something positive happens, you wonder if you deserved it, whether it was given to you by chance or to cover up a certain agenda. According to you, there is never a good enough reason to experience positivity.

Should Statements: Do you find yourself constantly living by "should" statements? For example, do you believe you "should" act a certain way or that those around you "should" also behave in a specific way? With this kind of thinking, you set expectations for both yourself and those around you. Then, when you're unable to live up to those statements, you begin to feel guilty and shameful. When another person does not do what you anticipate them to, you often find yourself disappointed or angry.

Labelling and Mislabelling: After a certain experience, you might find yourself using highly emotional, negative, senseless, and inaccurate words to label yourself, the people around you, or the situation at hand. You might call yourself a "fat face" when you're out shopping and if the jeans don't fit you or call a waiter that does not greet you back in high spirits a "tired, lazy fool."

Magnification (Catastrophizing) and Minimizing: Are you reading too much into situations? Do you find yourself creating a misinterpretation of your perspective by either magnifying or minimizing the meaning, importance, or effect of something? That is what this distortion is all about. You might get recognition at work for exceeding your sales target and still believe you're the worst salesperson they've ever hired. Or you might miss a target by a small margin and already start looking for another job because you're convinced you're going to get fired.

Mind Reading: Here, you're convinced to know what another person is thinking! Of course, it's possible to be able to take in hints about what another person might be thinking of doing or saying, but this type of extreme distortion only allows you to delve into negative interpretations which might sometimes be exaggerated.

Overgeneralizing: Based on one or two experiences from your past, you often conclude a simple situation into something that you're familiar with. Oftentimes, this generalizing of outcomes leads to you thinking negatively about yourself and those around you because you live by and only believe patterns. For example, if you've recently started seeing someone and they don't call you at the time they said they would, you might decide that they're no longer interested or that you're not worth a call simply because it has been done to you before.

Emotional Reasoning: Aren't we all guilty of this one? Here, you live by one distorted truth: If I feel it, then it's true! With this distortion, you become governed by your unreasonable emotions and will often take them as facts. If you feel like your partner is cheating, you start treating them differently simply because you can feel it. If you feel like your sister is going to disappoint you this coming weekend, you start acting weird around her, anticipating the fight that will ensue. It's an illogical way of thinking.

2. After picking your distortion (or distortions if you related to more than one), explain why they resonate with you more without giving any examples. Why do you believe this happens? How often does it happen? And why do you feel more comfortable relying on this type of thinking?

3. Give ten (or more) examples of when you adopted this way of thinking. Explain what happened, how it happened, and what happened when you applied this way of thinking. In your examples, ensure that you mention either your verbal negative self-talk, thoughts, or actions.

4. Write down ten (or more) negative self-beliefs that have not allowed you to be compassionate toward yourself. For example, you might believe you are destined for failure, that

you make a bad mother or wife, or that you're a disappointment to your parents.

5. For each point that you've identified in steps three and four, expand on it further by looking into:

- how you can change your irrational statements into more positive ones? It could be as simple as encouraging yourself to move from an "I am ugly" statement to "I am wonderfully and fearfully made."

- how you can adopt a new and different perspective when it comes to situations?

- whether there is any evidence for the facts that you've noted down.

- how you can use your distortion to create a different perspective? For example, with emotional reasoning, the first thing you can do after identifying an emotion is to allow yourself to investigate it and only react after you've found some credible facts. Or if you find yourself maximizing an event, speak about the situation you've found yourself in and investigate whether you're being reasonable or irrational. For example, if you did not meet your sales targets this year, the best thing to do would be to speak to your manager about it right? Find out what can be done, or how you can get support from your organization as opposed to just deciding to draft a resignation letter.

Exercise 12: The Compassionate Toolkit

This will probably be your favorite exercise and I understand why. While you might've learned the importance of being gentle with yourself, most of these exercises are internal work that requires you to do them away from practical experiences. With this one, I need you to refer back to the story about our friend Shinraku. When she was stuck in traffic, she engaged in something that all of us are guilty of. She neglected to be gentle with herself and settled for attacking herself, even though she had little control of the situation. Now, how many times has that happened to you before?

For this exercise, I need you to think of scenarios where you've found yourself being so frustrated that you also blamed yourself for situations that were out of your control. If you think of Shinraku, she obviously could not get herself a new car at that moment, but there are a few things that would've helped calm the situation or allowed her to take care of herself.

1. When looking at your unique situations that are similar to hers, what do you think could've helped you deal with unforeseen circumstances better? I need you to think of affordable, tangible, and helpful resources that you realize are easily accessible to you. For example, a box of tissues could help if you're an emotional person, maybe your battery once died, and you couldn't make any phone calls during that difficult time. In an instance like that, a car charger is something that you know is essential to your list. Write down all of these things that you know will be able to help you be gentle with yourself.
2. After formulating your list, go out there and ensure that you get all of the items you've noted in your list.
3. Get a nice box or bag that will accommodate all of the items you've bought. This will be known as your compassionate toolkit.
4. Ensure that you carry this box or bag with you wherever you go.
5. The next time you're in a challenging situation and you actively try to be gentle with yourself, make the situation easier by going into your toolkit and using an item that will remind you that you still need to put yourself first.
6. To ensure that you don't neglect this exercise, I need you to use one item per week, even though you might convince yourself that you're not necessarily in a challenging situation.
7. Once you've used the item, come back to your workbook and note down your experience. How did the toolkit help you? How did you feel after using it? And what has it taught you about compassion?

Make sure that your toolkit is always filled with all of the necessary items you've noted as needs. As time goes on, you might find yourself identifying other items that you need to buy to add to your box. When this happens, don't give in to the temptation of shrugging it off; your thoughts and feelings about these items are valid! Moreover, follow the final and most important rule: An item will only be removed from the toolkit once it has been used, not when you feel like it because you never know when you might need it in an emergency!

CHAPTER 4: Creating a Desired Reality With Affirmations

Don't be pushed around by the fears in your mind. Be led by the dreams in your heart.

- Roy T. Bennett

Although it might seem like affirmations have become the latest fad dominating social media, they've been around much longer than you think. Over and over again, we've heard some of the best-celebrated individuals making powerful statements that helped them create beautiful legacies for themselves, and of course, their loved ones! Before going into a boxing match, Muhammed Ali would refer to himself as "The greatest", and former first lady Michelle Obama uses the statement "Am I good enough? Yes, I am," (Borge, 2021, para. 8) to gain the courage to pursue the things that matter to her the most, no matter how challenging they might be. I've only made two examples, but I believe you understand just how empowering these statements are.

Through what these individuals declared about themselves, they were able to achieve feats that most people would never imagine that people of their caliber would be able to. Now I've got a good question for you: what statements about yourself are you using to build yourself up and create an unforgettable legacy?

What Are Affirmations?

An affirmation is a positive statement that challenges you to transform your negative mentality, anticipate a desired future, and motivate you to reach your full potential. We've all heard these kinds of statements before, but we've never really used them to our advantage. We often post quotes and statements that we find online that we feel energize us, but we never internalize them enough to understand that they have the power to become our reality.

Scientifically, the more you repeat these statements to yourself, the more you convince your subconscious mind that it's the absolute truth. Over time, your subconscious will believe these statements so much that it will propel you to actively make them a reality. In other words, affirmations will trigger you to quit bad habits, take better chances, and make all the necessary changes in your life for better results. They will make you feel good about yourself, resolve the trust issues that you have with yourself, and cause you to fall in love with yourself all over again.

What Makes an Affirmation?

Is there a formula to follow when formulating affirmations or choosing the right ones to recite? The answer is simple, yes!

Think of this statement: "I am deliberate and afraid of nothing," (Borge, 2021, para. 10). When you read it out loud, what kind of sensation or shift do you sense mentally, emotionally, and physically? Of course, you somehow start feeling like there's nothing to be afraid of. You believe in everything that you've been deliberate about, and you look forward to positive outcomes! In other words, an effective affirmation is:

- a positive statement is written in the positive and present tense. Most affirmations usually begin with "I am…"
- emotive. Meaning your statement should have a word that elicits some form of positive emotion. For example, "I am happy to…" "I am grateful for" or "I love that…"
- an indication of your desires: affirmations allow you to declare boldly what it is that you'd like to achieve or manifest into your reality
- certain: your statement moves with some sense of surety in it. Even if you might have a few doubts initially, you'll know after

reciting your statements a few times that there is power in what you're claiming.

In this chapter, we're going to use the power of affirmations to create a reality that you've always been yearning for. Slowly, you're going to reclaim your confidence and ability to reach for the stars by incorporating positive and powerful statements into your life.

Exercise 13: Shopping for Affirmations

I want to get you comfortable by getting you comfortable with affirmations that have worked for other well-known individuals that you look up to. In this exercise, you'll identify five personalities that inspire you. They could be successful entrepreneurs, people who motivate you to get fit and healthy, or simply someone who taught you that it's possible to overcome the kind of things you've also been through.

Do some research and write down the affirmations that your favorite personalities have believed in or used throughout their lives. Write them down in bold letters and spend the next five days meditating on these words. For a structured meditation session, think about:

- the emotion used in the statement, and how it makes you feel.
- what the statement allows the person to think of themselves and how this has contributed to their success.
- the actions that those affirmations have triggered the individuals to take.
- which areas of your life would you use these affirmations and what kind of changes do you believe you'd invite into your life?

That's it! After five days, you'll notice how confident you are in your ability to identify and denote positive statements. This exercise will also enlighten you about some unshakeable truth: there is power in the words you let out of your mouth! Once you have completed this exercise, move on to another one that requires you to use your creative juices!

_____

_____

_____

_____

_____

_____

_____

Exercise 14: Creating Your Own Affirmations

In this exciting step, you're going to use the formula mentioned above to create your affirmations. Follow the instructions below:

1. Identify the aspects of your life that you believe would benefit from affirmations. You can achieve this by looking into what dream you're trying to turn into reality. Do you want to pass your degree cum laude? Do you want to improve your body image? Are you looking to tackle your level of self-esteem? Write down what your deliberate intentions are.

2. Then, for each part of your life, write down a minimum of five affirmations that you believe can change your life. Remember

to be emotive, add conviction, that is, write them down as if they've already happened, and direct them to yourself in the present tense and with an active voice. Some affirmations will not necessarily start with "I am…" and that's okay, just ensure that they remain positive.

3. Now, pick an affirmation of the day that you're going to recite for a minimum of 21 days. Write it down on a sticky note and paste it where you'll see it throughout the day. Set it up as your status message on your social media platforms or make it your wallpaper on your cellphone so that you will always remember to recite it every time you hold your phone.

4. This is important: Believe what you're saying! Act it out if you have to, raise your voice louder, and use your body language to reaffirm your truth, but don't ever for a second cause your sub-conscious to question you by being doubtful!

5. By the 21st day, formulate an action plan that will gradually lead you into this desired reality. When you say, "I am more than grateful to pass my degree with distinction," then you've got to start acting like someone ready to graduate with distinc-tion! Work out a study plan, attend every class, and be an active participant during your classes. Although your subconscious is going to push you to do something about transforming your reality, you have the ultimate power to ensure that everything goes exactly as you plan it!

Exercise 15: Complete the Sentence

I want you to get comfortable with affirmations so much that you notice them even in the simplest conversations. This will trigger you to start being cautious about the things you utter with your mouth! Words indeed have power and can manifest themselves into reality. Therefore, I need you to investigate the questions below and answer them to create a truth around them. If you find yourself over-analyzing your answers, then good! It's a great indication that you're starting to pay special attention to how you perceive things, especially yourself.

You don't have to complete all the questions at once. You might choose to answer five a day or a week. Or you might take control of your day by completing a sentence each morning, it's entirely up to you. The rules are simple, in the questions, you either insert an emotion or a desired future.

1. I appreciate that I am...
2. Today, I gracefully choose self-love by...
3. I am... because I can...
4. I am proud of my...
5. I am... to be learning how to...
6. I feel blessed to be good at...

7. I am more than... I know I can...
8. Today is a... I am finally going to...
9. I am... Which is a...
10. I can... It's all under my control.
11. I am grateful for...
12. Today I gracefully choose self-care by...
13. Come rain or sunshine, it gives me great pleasure to know that...
14. I am blessed because...
15. I am thankful for...
16. I am... to be relearning how to...
17. When it comes to... I am happy to announce I am content, because I know I'm doing my best.
18. Today, I gracefully choose self-compassion by...
19. Today I will...
20. I believe I...
21. I am in control of... and that makes me...
22. Today, the universe will conspire for me to...
23. Do I deserve everything good that has come my way?
24. Today is all about...
25. I am a magnet for...
26. I'm... to be letting go of...
27. I... To set healthy boundaries
28. I am... To be aligned with...
29. Today I choose... as a love language.
30. To Doubt: I'm so ecstatic that I never have to... again!
31. To the inner critic: I'm so grateful...
32. Gratitude is...
33. I'm excited! My... is about to explode!
34. I deserve a... relationship
35. Finally, I'm... to...
36. I am unlearning...
37. To my younger self:...
38. I am kind to my...
39. I embrace...
40. I am getting... and... every day!
41. I attract...

42. I radiate…
43. Today is a good day to…
44. I am the master of my feelings, today I choose to feel…
45. Laughter is…
46. I'm allowed to…
47. When I walk into any room…
48. To self-loathing:…
49. I am humbled by…
50. Today I will love myself by…

Exercise 16: My Beautiful Future

Are you feeling blessed already? Well, this exercise is going to ensure that you continue to feel great about yourself and hope for the future.

This is a visualization exercise that is going to encourage you to use your imagination to generate positive feelings about your capabilities and your future. You're going to let go of what you've been through and where you are in life and finally focus on what matters most, which is where you're going! In the future, you're going to accomplish all your goals and turn all of your wildest dreams into a reality.

We are going to divide the exercise into three parts:

- **Your personal life:** This includes aspects of your life that matter to you the most. They should be solely focused on serving you and no one else. This could be your spiritual life, your desire to grow your EQ, improve your health, and gain financial independence.
- **Your professional life:** This aspect covers how you envision your career growth. Are you going to follow your dreams using your talent? Do you want to climb the corporate ladder? Or do you want to have the guts to change your career?
- **Your social life:** You're also going to look at the different kinds of relationships you have in your life and how you want them to change. Furthermore, you might also want to change the way you socialize with others. Perhaps you want to go out more often or spend more time with your loved ones as opposed to drowning yourself with work.

Steps:

1. For three weeks, you're going to visualize and note down the life you want to create yourself regarding these three parts of your life. The first week can be dedicated to your personal life, followed by the two topics I've mentioned above.

2. Dedicate about ten minutes to thinking about the life you want professionally, in your career, and personality. In each area of your life, how are you living your best possible life? What exactly are you doing, where are you doing it, and who are you doing it with?

3. Once you've thought about your pleasant future, write it all down and ensure that you're being specific about everything! If you're driving a new car, mention the model and color. If you're living in a new house, talk about how the house looks and where it's located.

You might be wondering what the purpose of this exercise is. If you're on a quest to fall in love with yourself, then why should you be indulging in wishful thinking? The answer is simple. There is power in visualization because it elicits incredible feelings about yourself and allows you to think freely about the beautiful things you deserve to have in your love. Most of the time, when people are struggling to appreciate themselves, they often develop a mentality that tells them that they should be settling, that they're incapable of achieving certain things, and that they're destined for failure. However, this exercise shows you your value and encourages you to chase wellness.

CHAPTER 5: The Power of Gratitude

I know for sure that appreciating whatever shows up for you in life changes your personal vibration. You radiate and generate more goodness for yourself when you're aware of all you have and not focusing on your have-nots.

- Oprah Winfrey

I f there's any woman who can teach us about the power of gratitude, it is Oprah Winfrey, a powerful business mogul who built herself from nothing but ensured that she acquired the life that she believed she deserves. You might be thinking, *how on earth should I express my gratitude if I have nothing to be grateful for?* Well, Oprah has an answer for you! While speaking to the graduating class of 2017 at Skidmore College 2017, she told them, "I practice being grateful. A lot of people say, 'Oh Oprah, that's easy for you 'cause you got everything!'" However, she argues that there's a reason for it. "I got everything because I practiced being grateful." (Ginsberg, 2017, para.14).

Oprah continues to support her claim by saying, "I know for sure that appreciating whatever shows up for you in life changes your personal vibration. You radiate and generate more goodness for yourself when you're aware of all you have and not focusing on your have-nots." (Mejia, 2018, para. 21). Does it still sound unbelievable to you?

Research shows that grateful people have a higher sense of self-esteem. Apart from the health benefits associated with being happy, the attitude of gratitude allows you to view people, the world, and yourself in a much more positive way. (Mendez, 2020a).

For you to develop a stronger appreciation of yourself, you've got to start appreciating and noticing the beautiful things that life continues to throw at you even on your worst days.

According to Dr. Meredith A. Pung, gratitude requires you to be intentional about noticing what is going on in and around you. "Taking time each day to actually write these things down can help you really reflect, savor, and feel the depth of your gratitude." (Mendez, 2020b, para. 3).

The exercises in this chapter are going to help you transform your mindset by shifting your perspective toward everything that is going well in your life, despite the fires that you might be trying to put out simultaneously. Practicing gratitude is a habit, meaning you've got to do it continuously until it becomes like second nature to you. There is power in not overthinking, faking, or downplaying it. It's a simple exercise that requires you to look around you and ask, *what good things have I got going on here?*

Are you ready to get started? Thank you!

Exercise 17: Developing an Attitude

Like most of the exercises in this book, this one will require you to commit to it on a long-term basis. Going back to Oprah Winfrey, the businesswoman says she kept gratitude for 20 years before she started neglecting it. It was in 1996 when she started feeling unhappy and unfulfilled, which was also strange because that is when she was at her busiest. She was making money, getting recognition for her work, and establishing her empire, but there was just this empty void inside of her that caused her to question herself. After some time, she reached a powerful conclusion: she was no longer practicing gratitude!

I'm not trying to say you're going to be unhappy the day you stop expressing gratitude. However, you should engage in this exercise for as long as you can to remain feeling positive and hopeful about your life. It will bring you a greater sense of appreciation and will make you fall in love with yourself, your life, and your surroundings, naturally so!

1. Every morning, state two things you woke up being grateful for. Don't overthink it. On some days you'll wake up being grateful for having a family and on some you'll be grateful for the sunshine! It's natural! Why are you grateful for this particular thing and what kind of positivity does it bring into your life?

2. In the evening, just before bedtime, reflect on two more things that you're grateful for. This time, you might want to think about the kind of day and your experiences. Continue to focus on why you're so grateful for those things and how they've made your life sweeter.

Gratitude by Mental Elimination:

1. After expressing your gratitude for three consecutive days, dedicate the next day to thinking about one good thing that you have in your life right now. It could be an event, a physical item, a relationship, or an individual.

2. For a minute or two, try to imagine what would happen to you or how you'd feel if you no longer had this one good thing. How miserable would you be? How would you cope? How different would your life be?

The second step might be upsetting, but according to research, when individuals are forced to mentally remove positive events, it improves their affective states, meaning their emotional states are the ones that will take a shift in perspective first. (Koo et al., 2008).

Exercise 18: Expressing Gratitude

In this exercise, you're going to shift your focus toward the items you mentioned in step 2 of the previous exercise. Looking at what you wrote, pick one person you'd like to thank. For example, you said you're grateful for having your mom in your life. You also wrote that you'd be nothing without her because she continues to take good care of you and your children. Tomorrow morning, make her day (and ultimately yours!) by sending her a nice message telling her exactly what you wrote down!

You'll never run out of things and people to be grateful for. So, send your messages every morning or every Monday (or any day of the week) and notice how your relationships will improve, you'll find yourself laughing more, and the world will be more beautiful for you.

Exercise 19: Making It Contagious!

Luckily for the entire world, gratitude is a contagious attitude and it's now your responsibility to ensure that it is present in the spaces you find yourself in!

1. In this exercise, think of a space where you want to spread this positive vibe to. It could be your home, your office, or even both, as long as it's an environment that allows you to be happy.
2. Then get a jar (which we'll call the gratitude jar), sticky notes, and a few pens that will help make this exercise a success.
3. Inform the people in your group that they are to write down a thing or a person that they're grateful for-they can do this once a day. Then, they should leave the note in the jar.
4. At the end of the week, during downtimes like lunch or family time, take turns to read a few notes that people have left in the jar. Every note is going to be worth it! Some will be funny, others will make you reflect, and some will encourage you to stop taking such special moments and bonds for granted. On some days, you're going to get the sweetest notes that will remind you just how amazing you are too!

Exercise 20: Practicing It Through the Power of Photography

It's no secret that art enables us to communicate things we wouldn't otherwise be able to communicate with our words. In this exercise, you're going to tap into the power of therapeutic photography. This is taking, analyzing, and using photography as a means to achieve healing, and growth, or express your gratitude using your surroundings.

It is also a form of mindfulness as it requires you to be present, aware of your surroundings, and intentional about your actions. This helps you to stay focused, calm your mind, and relieve stress. During a time of depression and anxiety, filmmaker and photographer Tara Wray used it as a powerful tool to help her cope. "It's like exercise: You don't want to do it, you have to make yourself do it, and you feel better after you do." (Harlan, 2018, para. 2). And she is correct! In 2010, researchers published a summary study titled *The Connection Between Art, Healing, and Public Health: A Review of Current Literature*, in which they looked at the effects of art on physical and psychological health. Unsurprisingly, they found that expressive art allows people to express themselves symbolically. Through this, people become more focused on positive things in their lives, rediscover their identity and self-worth, and report long-term improvements in their physical and mental health (Stuckey & Nobel, 2010). You're about to be blessed with these benefits too!

Please don't worry about your creative or photographic skills. Do not think about not having the latest camera or lighting. We just want to have fun and create special memories!

Steps:

1. Think of five things that you're grateful for in your life right now. If you're going to include people on this list, ensure that you write down why you're grateful for them and not just their names.
2. Dedicate a day or a few hours to going out in nature to take pictures that can explain better why you're grateful for the things you mentioned in step one. Please ensure that you go out when it's safe to and you go to an area that won't put your life or safety in danger.
3. The aim here is to tell a story through the power of photography, so take note of your surroundings and take powerful pictures! If for example, you're grateful for your existence, then you could take a picture of a beautiful sunrise setting to depict how humble you are to have been able to see another morning. If you're grateful for the peace and you believe that is better explained by showing your favorite morning drink, then go ahead and capture your beautiful mug and the hot steam that will be ready to dance for the camera!
4. Print out your photos and paste them into your workbook
5. For each picture or for every story that you tell through these photos, feel free to create a journal entry where you'll explain what the picture means, how you felt that day, and why you're grateful for those memories that you captured!

Conclusion

Congratulations, not only did you take an empowering step to learn how to love yourself again, but you committed to taking active measures that will ensure that you make compelling changes in your life.

Some women live their entire lives expecting to get adequate love and appreciation from their loved ones. It's a sensible expectation, but as you've learned, no one is going to commit to loving and appreciating the way you need to but you! I am more than confident in your ability to start valuing yourself. From the first exercise that you engage in, you will feel the power you've been suppressing for so long rise up and motivate you.

Reaching this page does not mean the journey to self-love has ended. I can guarantee you now that you'll wake up some days feeling like you're a failure. You'll convince yourself that some exercises are useless or that you just don't have it in you to get the desired results. Don't despair and don't feel guilty about feeling the need to revisit some chapters just to energize yourself again. This is your workbook, and it's going to serve you for as long as you allow it to!

Remember that you are going to experience a lot of resistance from the people around you. You will shock them every time you say no, establish a boundary, or call someone out for not treating them right. You will feel guilty about it, but you'll enjoy being in improved relationships and having the ability to have things happening on your terms and conditions. So no matter how tough it gets, you cannot allow yourself to disappoint yourself!

Even when you disappoint yourself, never forget the lessons you learned about self-compassion. You are worthy of good treatment, gentle words, and self-care! Indulge in taking care of yourself, your me time, and getting help from others.

If you find yourself enjoying a particular exercise that you only intended to do for a limited amount of time, feel free to extend the duration of the exercise, and remember not to overthink anything!

From now on, may you never take for granted the things you have around you, the power you carry within you, and the beautiful future you're going to create with the power of your words! State your intentions with conviction and then go out there to execute them gracefully.

FREE GIFT

Greetings!

First of all, we want to thank you for reading our books. We aim to create the very best books for our readers.

Now we invite you to join our exclusive list. As a subscriber, you will receive a free gift, weekly tips, free giveaways, discounts and so much more.

<u>All of this is 100% free with no strings attached!</u>

To claim your bonus simply head to the link below or scan the QR code below.

RELOVEPSYCHOLOGY

https://www.subscribepage.com/relovepsychology

SELF-LOVE WORKBOOK FOR WOMEN

We sincerely hope you enjoyed our new book *"Self-Love Workbook for Women"*. We would greatly appreciate your feedback with an honest review at the place of purchase.

First and foremost, we are always looking to grow and improve as a team. It is reassuring to hear what works, as well as receive constructive feedback on what should improve. Second, starting out as an unknown author is exceedingly difficult, and Amazon reviews go a long way toward making the journey out of anonymity possible. Please take a few minutes to write an honest review.

Best regards,

Relove Psychology

http://relovepsychology.com/

References

Ackerman, C. (2017, September 29). *Cognitive Distortions: When Your Brain Lies to You* (+ PDF Worksheets). PositivePsychology.com. https://positivepsychology. com/cognitive-distortions/

Amberly, & Joe. (2020, September 18). *50 Ways to Speak Love Using Physical Touch.* Aprioritizedmarriage.com. https://aprioritizedmarriage.com/blog/physical-touch-love-language-examples/

B.Sc, E. H. (2019, September 30). *19 Top Positive Psychology Exercises for Clients or Students.* PositivePsychology.com. https://positivepsychology.com/positive-psychology-exercises/#6

Baikie, K. A., & Wilhelm, K. (2005). Emotional and physical health benefits of expressive writing. *Advances in Psychiatric Treatment,* 11(5), 338–346. https://doi. org/10.1192/apt.11.5.338

Baker, C. (n.d.). *9 Self-Esteem Boosting Exercises to Try* | SkillsYouNeed. Www. skillsyouneed.com. https://www.skillsyouneed.com/rhubarb/self-esteem-exercises .html

Borge, J. (2021, May 19). *40 Positive Affirmations for a Sunnier Outlook.* Oprah Daily. https:// www.oprahdaily.com/life/relationships-love/g25629970/positive-affirmations/ ?slide=10

CFI Team. (2022, May 7). *SMART Goal - Definition, Guide, and Importance of Goal Setting.* Corporate Finance Institute. https://corporatefinanceinstitute.com/resources/knowledge/other/smart-goal/

Cherry, K. (2021, February 17). *How to Forgive Yourself. Verywell Mind.* https://www. verywellmind.com/how-to-forgive-yourself-4583819#:~:text=Forgiveness%20 is%20often%20defined%20as

Creatio. (2021, July 12). *The Importance of Affirmations.* The Y. https://www.ymcansw. org.au/news-and-media/the-y-at-home/the-importance-of-affirmations/

Crosley, H. (2010, February 10). *Beyonce Says She "Killed" Sasha Fierce.* MTV. https:// www.mtv.com/news/13z2bh/beyonce-says-she-killed-sasha-fierce

Falconer, E. (2015, May 14). *5 Reasons to Write a Letter to Yourself (and How to Do It)*. Pick the Brain | Motivation and Self Improvement. https://www.pickthebrain. com/blog/5-reasons-write-letter/

French Dunbar, M. (n.d.). *What Is a Purposeful Life and How Do I Get One?* Meghan French Dunbar. Retrieved August 21, 2022, from https://www.meghanfrenchdunbar.com/blog/what-is-a-purposeful-life-and-how-do-i-get-one

FTD FRESH. (2020, January 11). *25+ Love Language Ideas For Your Significant Other, Your Kids & Yourself.* FTD.com. https://www.ftd.com/blog/celebrate/ love-language-ideas

Ginsberg, L. (2017, May 23). *According to Oprah Winfrey, these are the 4 things you need to know to be successful.* CNBC. https://www.cnbc.com/2017/05/23/oprah-winfrey-these-are-the-4-things-you-need-to-know-for-success.html

Goodreads. (2009). *Self Esteem Quotes* (2407 quotes). Goodreads.com. https://www. goodreads.com/quotes/tag/self-esteem

Hamilton, D. (2016, September 9). *How to use visualisation to boost your self-love.* David R Hamilton PHD. https://drdavidhamilton.com/how-to-use-visualisation-to-boost-your-self-love/

Harlan, B. (2018, December 31). *Channeling The Pain Of Depression Into Photography, And Finding You Are Not Alone.* NPR.org. https://www.npr.org/sections/ pictureshow/2018/12/31/677341382/one-photographers-message-if-you-feel-too-tired-you-re-not-alone

Hasseldine, R. (2015, June 22). *Why Do Women Find It So Difficult to Put Themselves First?* HuffPost. https://www.huffpost.com/entry/why-do-women-find-it-so-d_ b_7621976

Hay, L. L. (2017). *You can heal your life.* Sydney Hay House, Inc.

Kholghi, B. (2020, June 5). *5 Best Setting Boundaries Exercises PDF.* Coaching-Online. org. https://www.coaching-online.org/5-best-setting-boundaries-exercises-pdf/

Koo, M., Algoe, S. B., Wilson, T. D., & Gilbert, D. T. (2008). It's a wonderful life: Mentally subtracting positive events improves people's affective states, contrary to their affective forecasts. *Journal of Personality and Social Psychology*, 95(5), 1217– 1224. https://doi.org/10.1037/a0013316

Ltd, T. B. S. I. (2021, March 8). *Self Love Crisis: 1 in 2 Women Worldwide Feel More Self-doubt Than Self-love.* Www.prnewswire.com. https://www.prnewswire.com/ news-releases/self-love-crisis-1-in-2-women-worldwide-feel-more-self-doubt-than-self-love-301241851.html#:~:text=37%25%20of%20single%20 women%2C%20and

Mani, M. (2019, April 17). *36 Inspirational Quotes On Why You Should Always Put Yourself First.* OutofStress.com. https://www.outofstress.com/inspirational-quotes-about-putting-yourself-first/

Mejia, Z. (2018, February 16). *How Arianna Huffington, Tony Robbins and Oprah Winfrey use gratitude as a strategy for success.* CNBC. https://www.cnbc.com/2018/02/16/ how-arianna-huffington-tony-robbins-and-oprah-use-gratitude-to-succeed.html#: ~:text=%E2%80%9CI%20practice%20being%20grateful%2C%E2%8 0%9D

Mendez, M. K., Mayra. (2020a, December 15). *5 easy ways to practice gratitude and make giving thanks part of your daily routine.* Insider. https://www.insider.com/ guides/health/mental-health/how-to-practice-gratitude

Mendez, M. K., Mayra. (2020b, December 15). *5 science-backed benefits of gratitude for your physical health, relationships, self-esteem, and more.* Insider. https://www.insider. com/guides/health/mental-health/benefits-of-gratitude#:~:text=Gratitude%20 increases%20self%2Desteem

Moore, C. (2019, March 4). *Positive Daily Affirmations: Is There Science Behind It?* PositivePsychology.com. https://positivepsychology.com/daily-affirmations/ #positive-affirmations

Mustafa, T. (2021, March 9). *Global study reveals half of women feel more self-doubt than self-love.* Metro. https://metro.co.uk/2021/03/09/global-study-reveals-half-of-women-feel-more-self-doubt-than-self-love-14213400/

Rezvani, S. (2021, December 14). *Over-explaining hurts your confidence . Here's how to stop!* Www.linkedin.com. https://www.linkedin.com/pulse/over-explaining-hurts-your-confidence-heres-how-stop-selena/

Ross, K. (2017, September 6). *You need to put yourself first but why is it so hard?* Start with You. https://www.startwithyou.co/blog/putting-yourself-first/#:~:text=Putting%20 yourself%20first%20doesn

Shinraku, L. S. (2013, May 21). *A Powerful Lesson in Self-Compassion: Are You Allergic to Honey?* Tiny Buddha. https://tinybuddha.com/blog/a-powerful-lesson-in-self-compassion-are-you-allergic-to-honey/

Stafford, K. (2016, December 1). *4 Health Benefits of Giving to Others.* Www.conehealth.com. https://www.conehealth.com/services/behavioral-health/4-health-benefits-of-giving-to-others-/#:~:text=Giving%20has%20been%20proven%20to

Stallings, A. (2022, April 22). *Beyonce Once Revealed That Her Alter-Ego Interfered With Her Performance With Prince.* Showbiz Cheat Sheet. https://www.cheatsheet.com/ entertainment/beyonce-revealed-alter-ego-interfered-performance-prince.html/

Stuckey, H. L., & Nobel, J. (2010). The Connection Between Art, Healing, and Public Health: A Review of Current Literature. *American Journal of Public Health,* 100(2), 254–263. https://doi.org/10.2105/ajph.2008.156497

The One Project. (2018). *Therapeutic Photography - Using Photography as Therapy.* The One Project. https://theoneproject.co/therapeutic-photography/

Van Edwards, V. (2020, October 4). *Take The Love Language Quiz and Find Your Love Language.* Science of People. https://www.scienceofpeople.com/ love-language-quiz-list/

Zameena Mejia. (2018, February 16). *How Arianna Huffington, Tony Robbins and Oprah Winfrey use gratitude as a strategy for success.* CNBC; CNBC. https://www. cnbc.com/2018/02/16/how-arianna-huffington-tony-robbins-and-oprah-use-gratitude-to-succeed.html